# BRADWELL
## THEN & NOW
### IN COLOUR

MARION HILL

The
History
Press

First published in 2011

The History Press
The Mill, Brimscombe Port
Stroud, Gloucestershire, GL5 2QG
www.thehistorypress.co.uk

British Library Cataloguing in Publication Data.
A catalogue record for this book is available from the British Library.

ISBN 978 0 7524 6319 3

Typesetting and origination by The History Press
Production managed by Jellyfish Print Solutions and manufactured in India

# CONTENTS

# ACKNOWLEDGEMENTS

With thanks for permission to use photographs from the publication *Bradwell Past and Present* (Sutton, 1997) that are reprinted in this edition: Bucks County Council Centre for Buckinghamshire Studies (www.buckscc.gov.uk/sites/bcc/archives/Centre_for_Buckinghamshire_Studies.page); Commission for the New Towns (which became English Partnerships, which itself became the Homes and Community Agency); Mrs Kitchener, daughter-in-law of the late Maurice Kitchener; Living Archive (www.livingarchive.org.uk); Milton Keynes City Discovery Centre (www.mkcdc.org.uk); Milton Keynes Museum (www.mkmuseum.org.uk); Wolverton & District Archaeological Society (www.mkheritage.co.uk/wdahs)

With thanks for updated or further information included in this edition: Bradwell Parish websites (www.bradwell-pc.gov.uk); Bradwell Silver Band (www.bradwellband.co.uk); 'Clutch Club' websites (http://clutch.open.ac.uk/schools) – 'Computer Literacy and Understanding through Communicating History' – researches from a project for website creation by parents and children in sixty schools within 30 miles' radius of Milton Keynes, run by Living Archive and the Open University; Bryan Dunleavy's memories (http://wolvertonpast.blogspot.com); Bob Hill, for nearly all the modern photographs; Living Archive interviews and transcripts with residents from across the Milton Keynes area; and Living Archive linked heritage websites, created by customised IT training courses (My Heritage; My Recollections; My Memories; My Home Front; My Webpage, all accessed via www.livingarchive.org); Milton Keynes Council (www.milton-keynes.gov.uk); Milton Keynes Heritage Association website (www.mkheritage.co.uk) especially Sue Blake's research on Haversham (www.mkheritage.co.uk/hav/); Denis Mynard's archaeology papers which began under Milton Keynes Development Corporation (until 1984) and continued with Bucks County Council; New Bradwell Heritage Group (www.mkheritage.co.uk/nbhg), especially Jennifer Cooper.

# ABOUT THE AUTHOR

Marion Hill is passionate about Milton Keynes. A Londoner by birth, she came to the designated new city in 1972, and has lived and worked in the area ever since. She has written sixteen books including a 'docu-fiction' about a double murder in early twentieth-century Basildon and the detailed history of a Jacobean mansion in Hertfordshire. Ten of her books are about Milton Keynes, including *Bletchley Park People*, *Memories of Milton Keynes*, *Milton Keynes: a History and Celebration* and most recently *Calverton Manor Farm – a century of memories*. Much of the inspiration for Marion's local history books comes from the massive archive of people's reminiscences, photographs and memorabilia held at Living Archive, Milton Keynes – a celebrated model for community projects throughout the country and beyond.

# INTRODUCTION

The name of Bradwell covers perhaps one of the most confusingly labelled and disparate geographical areas in the new city of Milton Keynes: New Bradwell was created over a century-and-a-half ago, along with Wolverton, the world's first-ever customised 'new town'. However, locals continued to call New Bradwell 'Stantonbury' well into the 1930s, even though the once-nearby village of Stanton itself ceased to function around 400 years before that.

Old Bradwell assumed its venerable prefix only in 1840 even though the village is in the Domesday Book of 1086, having been part of a gift from William the Conqueror to Walter Giffard, Lord of Longueville, for commanding his Norman army in Hastings. However, 'old' was dropped from the name in the twentieth century when Bradwell was incorporated into the grid square system of Milton Keynes, and despite the many wells in the village, locals have stubbornly called it 'Braddle'.

The modern Bradwell parish includes the new city estates of Heelands and Rooksley – both named after ancient fields. But neighbouring grid squares have strong demographic and historical links with 'Bradwell': the adjacent Roman site of Bancroft villa; the nearby 1930s estate of Bradville, named after Cadbury's Bournville village; and the 170-year-old Blue Bridge straddling the country's first north-to-south railway on which much of the area's development depended. Furthermore, despite their names, Bradwell Abbey hosts a large industrial estate and Bradwell Common is home to several popular housing estates.

This whole area is intersected by the ancient Bradwell Brook, crossed by Roman tracks, dissected by the eighteenth-century Grand Union Canal, sliced by the nineteenth-century London to Birmingham railway and newly sectioned by the late twentieth-century city grid-road system – the vertical bisection, north to south, of Grafton Street (V6), and the horizontal ones, west to east, of Millers Way (H2), Monks Way (H3), and Dansteed Way (H4).

However, in these same physical divisions and labels lie the historical secrets which unite them. From fragments of Bronze Age implements of 2000 BC in the New Bradwell area to the disused Wolverton to Newport Pagnell railway branch line threading its modern route as a cycle and pedestrian Redway, this Bradwell land is a microcosm of English history evidenced from the earliest settlers.

Although some of the older images in this book themselves may have existed for a little more than 100 years, the pictures and stories bear witness to nearly 4,000 years of local life. Browse, celebrate our special city heritage and enjoy!

# LOUGHTON ROAD, BRADWELL VILLAGE

LOUGHTON ROAD MARKS the eastern edge of Bradwell Village. As one of the four sides of the village's square of roads (with Vicarage, Primrose and Abbey roads), Loughton Road in this image is from the north *c*.1910. At the top of the road on the west was the infants' school, built by the

London and North Western Railway Company in 1891 to accommodate sixty children of its employees at Wolverton Works. The old school had closed in 1876 forcing a mile-long walk into New Bradwell. 'The road being a very bleak one, it was felt to be a great hardship of the infants', commented the *Bucks Standard* in 1891.

A CENTURY LATER, despite the growth of the new city around it, little more than the road layout, the trees and the form of transport seem to have changed. Loughton Road used to continue north as Bradwell Road in New Bradwell, but this connection was necessarily severed by the city grid road roundabout at Monks Way (H3) and Grafton Street (V6). However, the city's unique Redway footpath and cycle way follows the old route. Although the original infants' school closed in 1957 and the building is now a private residence, the city's new Bradwell Village School is thriving, with a total of 236 pupils as of 2009.

# PROVIDENCE PLACE, BRADWELL VILLAGE

PROVIDENCE PLACE IN Loughton Road is the site of this Scouts' gathering *c.*1930, close to the Methodist chapel. There had been a 'preaching station' in the village, initiated by Revd William

Bull of Newport Pagnell, since the eighteenth century. Opening in 1823 as a venue for 'dissenting religion', the chapel was described in *Sheahan's Guide* of 1861 as 'small and neat'. Although the chapel itself went through a period of disuse during the nineteenth century, by the 1880s there was an active Methodist following with over forty children enrolled in the Sunday school.

LATER, PROVIDENCE PLACE would see people arriving at the chapel for weddings, concerts, magic lantern shows and even the small library there. Electric lights arrived in 1933, although worshippers had to wait until 1963 for heating. By 1973, there were only three ageing members of the chapel left, but with the help of the Bradwell parish churches, and the energy of the new city, the 1980s brought new life, especially to the chapel floor whose original wooden tiles had been laid directly onto the soil! Now neighbouring Providence Place is grassed over and is lined with new housing, though the quiet remains.

9

# THATCHED COTTAGES, BRADWELL VILLAGE

THESE LISTED THATCHED cottages in Loughton Road were photographed *c.*1930 (right). Typical of north Buckinghamshire villages, such cottages would have originally been the dwellings of local artisans. For example Bradwell's 1798 *Posse Comitatus* (partial census) recorded thirty-seven families, which included four stonemasons, two cordwainers (shoemakers), a ratcatcher and a 'haggle cartman' – the only travelling salesman in the Newport area! By 1864, the village also had a carpenter, blacksmith, butcher, shopkeeper, two beer retailers and four farmers, one of whom was also a baker. At the end of the nineteenth century, 493 people lived in the village.

IN THE EARLY twentieth century, the parish covered 917 acres, 85 per cent of them used for agriculture – growing wheat, oats, barley and beans. By 1989, the estimated Bradwell population was 3,080. The civil parish currently consists of the Bradwell village grid square along with Heelands, Rooksley and Bradwell Common. It is bounded by the railway to the west, Monks Way (H3) to the north, Saxon Street (V7) to the east and Portway (H5) to the south. According to the 2001 census, its population was 9,389. These listed cottages have found new life with the new city: they are rethatched, with stone repointed and wood repainted.

# THE VICTORIA INN,
# BRADWELL VILLAGE

THE VICTORIA INN (photograph *c.*1950) seems to have once been Newman's Farm, mentioned in a property sale of 27 February 1639. But the nineteenth century saw it undergo a change of use: by 1876 *Harrods Guide* lists E. Bird as the landlord. At a 'smoking concert' of the Conservative Association held there in June 1892, Farmer Wylie reported having given his first vote to Disraeli in 1860 when there were only twenty voters; now, he said, there were 600. Later that year, the pub hosted the annual dinner of the village cricket club for forty guests, while Charles Sambrook declared that 'all the bellringers went to the Victoria'.

THE VICTORIA INN is now a listed building within the Old Bradwell conservation area, famous in the city for its Good Friday 'Beer and Bun Race'. Founded *c.*1965 by three residents – Messrs Smith, Johnson and Chapman – the race involves running round the village with a glass of beer in one hand and a bun in the other, the winner being whoever returns with the most beer. Runners are disqualified if they exceed the time limit (seven minutes for men, nine for women); or if they carry the bun in their mouths with a hand over the beer; or if friends top up the beer before they reach the finishing line!

# VICARAGE ROAD, BRADWELL VILLAGE

A VIEW OF Vicarage Road looking towards Loughton Road *c.*1935. The Victoria Inn sign can be seen on the left with the Prince Albert pub sign on the right. The lorry is delivering ale from Phipps Brewery, which had set up business in Northampton in 1817 after Pickering Phipps first brewed

beer in Towcester in 1801. The company enjoyed its heyday from 1920–50, taking over local breweries such as Hipwell of Olney, Eadley and Dulley of Market Harborough, and Campbell Praed of Wellingborough. But in 1960 it was itself subsumed by larger breweries and by the 1970s, its traditional brew had disappeared.

A SIMILAR VIEW today shows both pubs still in operation, although the terraced housing on the left has been replaced. The Victoria Inn now sells a modern resurrection of the old brand – Phipps IPA; the Prince Albert pub, also a listed building, stocks Wells' real ale brews as well as offering modern pub entertainment including quiz nights and live music. Vicarage Road contains no less than eleven of the twenty-one listed buildings in the village. One of them, which was once the Manor Farmhouse in 1790, is now a youth hostel. Others include the seventeenth-century 'Old Sugar Loaf' (No. 1) and No. 4 and No. 36 – both over 200 years old.

# THE BUS STOP, BRADWELL VILLAGE

THE VILLAGE BUS stop outside the Prince Albert pub (*c.* 1950) must have been a lifeline for villagers. The bus is thought to be a Crossley double-decker run by Wesley's Buses of Stoke Goldington and Newport Pagnell. These ladies are perhaps returning home from working as seamstresses at Wolverton Works or Salmons Coachworks in Newport Pagnell. Perhaps they worked at McCorquodale's printers or Taylors Mustard Factory. Special shopping trips might have been to the big Co-op department store in Bletchley, or Odell's ironmongers in Stony, or the

electricity and gas showrooms in Wolverton. Downstairs passengers on the bus were told: 'No spitting or smoking allowed.'

NOW BUSES NO longer stop in this little lane, although the view is much spruced up, with even Albert taking a different perspective! The first motor bus service in the country was introduced between Newport Pagnell and Olney in 1898, contributing to the demise of local railways; local bus routes still include nearby Bradville and New Bradwell. But with private transport now the preferred norm, the city's local centres can be accessed in every city grid square via the Redway cycle paths, and one of the largest shopping centres in Europe (with plentiful parking) is just five minutes' drive away.

# THE BRADWELL MOTTE

THE BRADWELL MOTTE is close to the church and Memorial Hall. This ancient earthwork is 22m in diameter reaching 2.3m high. Its dents are thought to have been made by attempts to construct an air-raid shelter during the Second World War. The remains of a surrounding ditch are 5m wide and 0.3m deep. A small bailey – or castle wall – can be seen 'up to 0.7m high, running for a distance of 36m some 20m from the mound edge'. A listed medieval fortified site, the original timber castle may well have been built in a period 900 years ago under King Stephen's reign, known as 'the anarchy'.

MORE RECENTLY, THE Bradwell Motte has seen a modern form of pleasurable anarchy in the form of the Bradwell Village Fête, run very successfully by the Bradwell Village Residents' Association in 2009. In its short life from 2005, the association regularly delivered 1,200 newsletters and put on public meetings with 'interesting local speakers', but with only a few organisers, energies were depleted and the association ceased. Despite this, residents' concerns continue to be catered for by a 'very active' Neighbourhood Action Group. Today, the motte is part of the village's public open space with the Memorial Hall still in view top left.

# THE MEMORIAL HALL, BRADWELL VILLAGE

LAYING THE FOUNDATION stone of the Memorial Hall, 1923. In the early years the main activities in this community hall were dances, whist drives and a film show twice a week. Its original inspiration – local men who served in the Great War – includes some poignant stories. Five

members of the Foolkes family alone went to war in 1914 with one, Frank, listed as 'fallen' on a plaque alongside the hall doors. The parents of Pte Walters of 9 Vicarage Road were offered some consolation by his Commanding Officer in that, unlike many of the 'fallen', at least 'his grave is marked and his rifle laid out on it...'

NOW THE MEMORIAL Hall (top right in the modern photograph) hosts Scottish country dancing, girls' choir, Weightwatchers, martial arts classes and the weekday preschool. The seventeenth-century Bradwell Manor farmhouse (left in the modern picture) was originally thatched, with a 'nag' house, 'gig' house, pig house, 'chaff' house, hen house, carthorse stable, granary and drying kiln. Now as a youth hostel (thirty-seven beds in seven rooms), it is on the Sustrans (sustainable transport) countrywide cycle network. In Milton Keynes, cyclists have 270km of customised city Redways, away from traffic and connecting with the North Bucks Way at Wolverton, the Three Shires Way at Tathall End and Swan's Way at Salcey Forest.

# ST LAWRENCE'S CHURCH, BRADWELL VILLAGE

ST LAWRENCE'S CHURCH, seen here *c.*1900, was acquired by Tickford Priory in Newport Pagnell in 1275. A listed building mainly originating from the thirteenth century, the church's

'saddleback' roof was incorporated into the rebuilding of the church in 1646. Its churchyard gate, along with the village pump, was built at the famed local ironworks of E. and H. Roberts of Deanshanger in 1821. Nineteenth-century tourists were urged to pause on their travels to see the church: the *Sheahan Guide* of 1861 describes it as 'an ancient and venerable structure... Its tower contains four bells.'

'THE BELLS ARE still giving a joyful sound every Sunday and every Wednesday night for choir practice,' said Gillian Carey in an interview for the Clutch project in 2000. 'One of the original thirteenth century bells is in the south aisle of the church for all to see. It had a large crack in it, so that when it rang, it gave an odd sound, but now the whole peal of bells rings out sweetly and calls people to church every week.' The modern picture shows some architectural features removed (a door and railings), some replaced (a cross instead of a chimney) and some added (a window and extra drainpipes).

23

# THE BRADWELL STOCKS

THE BRADWELL STOCKS *c.*1900: The medieval village stocks stood on the small green at the western end of Primrose Road. Originally designed to confine miscreants by restraining their legs (so they could be pelted with rotten food), these stocks were among the last to survive in the country – apparently still there in 1945. One wrong-doer in the early twelfth century ended up with a harsher punishment. According to the law-court records of 1227: 'Adam de Bradwelle killed Robert Le Marchaunt and fled to the Church and abjured the realm.' He was captured, tried and publicly hanged.

THE SITE OF the Bradwell Stocks, 2011. The tree was planted for the Queen's Jubilee in 1977 by Alderman Ray Bellchambers OBE JP (1919–2007). Much respected city-wide, he helped plan the original concept of Milton Keynes, serving on the Development Corporation Board for sixteen years from its inception in 1967. Governor of Radcliffe School, involved in the founding of Stantonbury Campus and the restoration of Bradwell Abbey, he was part-founder of the City Discovery Centre and of Milton Keynes Museum of which he became president. He acted as secretary of Bradwell Charities for thirty-two years, and Brian King from Bradwell Parish Council described him as: 'an enlightened champion of the Bradwell Parish community.'

# BRADWELL BURY
# MOAT HOUSE

THE BRADWELL BURY Moat House, the remains of which are shown here in 1975, was a thirteenth-century stone house that replaced the wooden structures of an earlier building, by then already around 300 years old. Centrally located within a rectangular moat, the house, which apparently went out of use in the fourteenth century, was described by D. Mynard in 1994 as: 'a high quality building of limestone, rubble-faced with dressed stone, with a tiled roof and at least one decorated tile floor. A stone barn and two stone circular dovecotes were located nearby. The finds, including imported pottery and a chess piece, suggest that it was the home of a wealthy person.'

TODAY THE BRADWELL Bury – or 'Braddlebury' – is covered by a sports field, its function a world away from that of the 'wealthy person' who lived there previously. Having been excavated and catalogued by Milton Keynes Development Corporation archaeologists in 1975, the site now hosts football and cricket (which has been played in the village for over 100 years), bowls and tennis. In the pavilion there is also a bar and a social club which hosts darts, dominoes and cribbage events.

# BRADWELL ABBEY
# CHAPEL OF ST MARY

IN 1155, A Benedictine priory was founded by Meinfelin, the Lord of Wolverton, but all that remains now are its moat, fishponds and the Grade I listed fourteenth-century Pilgrims' Chapel of St Mary. The priory monks believed that the figure of the Virgin Mary in a niche on the west front

of their church had miraculous healing qualities, so they enclosed it within the protective building of the chapel. Wall paintings date from 1350, and the floor tiles are believed to be from Little Brickhill 600 years ago. The left-hand picture is from 1981 after renovation by Milton Keynes Development Corporation.

TODAY, THE CHAPEL looks little changed. Trains still speed past on the main railway line behind it, as they have done for the last 170 years. But the nearby seventeenth-century Bradwell Abbey Manor farmhouse metamorphosed from the 1666 country residence of Sir Joseph Alston to the 1971 Bradwell Abbey Archaeological Field Centre, supported by Milton Keynes Development Corporation. Now the base for Milton Keynes City Discovery Centre, it provides courses and primary reference material on the unique provenance of our city development – as evidenced by the new city industrial estate that surrounds it.
*(Photograph reproduced with kind permission of Henk van Aswegan)*

# BRADWELL COMMON

BRADWELL COMMON'S HOMEWORLD 81 play area, 1981. When Alfred the Great ruled 1,200 years ago, the county divisions of England were composed of hundreds – land inhabited by 100 households. The meeting place of each hundred was generally on high ground, with a protective covering of trees. Here, justice was administered, property sales took place and political issues were debated. 'Sigelai', or the Secklow Hundred in which Bradwell Village was situated, was on

Bradwell Common. Two earlier Roman roads or tracks probably crossed here, from modern Stantonbury through Woughton, Simpson and to Fenny Stratford; and from Shenley through Loughton to Willen.

BRADWELL COMMON'S HOUSING came to national attention when Homeworld 81 opened on the site. Coleshill Place became renowned for the exhibition of innovative house building there. Twenty architects and developers from five countries were invited by Milton Keynes Development Corporation to design thirty-six dwellings. Among them were the BBC Money Programme 2000 House (No. 4), Ideal Homes Solar House (No. 5) and the Askeryd Pyramid (No. 36). By 1988, Bradwell Common, in line with other city grid squares, had its own new local centre with a combined school, local park, shops and pub – and a modern meeting place.

# BANCROFT ROMAN VILLA

VISITORS TO THE villa site, photographed in 1977. Around 900 BC, a Bronze Age family initiated nearly 3,000 years of continuous settlement at Bancroft when they built a large circular timber house. However, the site is nationally famous for the Roman villa farm built on top of it. The earliest known house in Milton Keynes, it is one of the largest of its kind, and its excavations are among the most extensive in the country. Soon after Julius Caesar had successfully invaded Britain (AD 52), the newly arrived settlers built a house from local limestone, with painted murals and a lavish bath suite of terracotta tiles.

TODAY, VISITORS TO the Bancroft Roman villa can see evidence of successive residents' formal gardens, summer house, ornamental pond and mosaics – one of which has been on long-term display in Queen's Court, central Milton Keynes. By the fourth century AD they had also left behind – possibly in a hurry – their coins, jewellery, pots, a board game and even an old shoe, size 41 (7½). The villa site was incorporated into the city's Linear Park by Milton Keynes Development Corporation. This park comprises a fifth of the whole city area exclusively assigned to public open space with leisure paths, cycle trails and picnic sites.

# BLUE BRIDGE

BLUE BRIDGE LOOKING west towards Loughton. Close to Bancroft, this famous railway bridge takes its name from the distinctive blue bricks used to build it 170 years ago. The original bridge, seen here (above) in 1997, was the site of a local tragedy on 5 June 1847, when the pointsman on duty there, Bernard Fossey, was responsible for a horrific accident at nearby Wolverton. He had apparently switched the London mail train into a goods siding where it crashed into some coal wagons, killing seven people and injuring many more.

BLUE BRIDGE TODAY stands amid new settlement construction, just as it did with the original nineteenth-century 'new towns' of Wolverton and New Bradwell. In the 1840s, the London and North Western Railway Company sank two wells near Blue Bridge for residents' water supply. It was pumped to two tanks at the top of Wolverton and gravity-fed to both communities. A busy city grid road runs parallel to the bridge in a horizontal line across the city – H2 Millers Way crosses both the railway and North Loughton Valley Park. This is another of the city's public spaces which is overseen by the Parks Trust and which controls floodwater with its 'wet/dry balancing lake'.

# BRADWELL WINDMILL

THE BRADWELL WINDMILL (photo *c.*1910) had a working life of only half a century. Shortly after the Cosgrove-Buckingham canal branch line opened in 1801, Samuel Holman bought an acre of land known as the Yawles from Henry Wilmin, so as to erect a mill and capitalise on the canal's new commercial prospects. A tower windmill was built in local stone in 1815 costing £500 with blades and sailcloths 52ft (17m) in diameter. The mill was bought in 1857 by Robert Adams

of Bradwell Abbey, but by 1864, after John Abbott bought it for £422 10s, the sails had revolved commercially for the last time.

IN MORE RECENT times, one local remembered 'climbing up through wooden floors on creaking, dusty, half-rotten steps right to the cap.' In 1949 however, the Wolverton Urban District Council recognised it as an important pre-industrial monument and it narrowly escaped demolition to be partially restored instead. In 1967 a tremendous gale blew one of the sails off; the other was hastily dismantled as a precaution. But in the early 1970s Milton Keynes Development Corporation bought it – for £10! – and restored it to full working order. Now having enjoyed the attention of the Friends of Bradwell Windmill, it is again protected, this time under the auspices of Milton Keynes Museum.

# THE BRADVILLE ESTATE

THE ORIGINAL BRADVILLE Estate, built by Wolverton Urban District Council, is shown here (right) at the junction of Bradwell Road and Abbey Way in a 1930s view taken by the eminent local photographer Maurice Kitchener. Residents first moved in when the road was still muddied, but deliveries helped: 'Milk was measured out, the Co-op breadman came, Herrington came from Loughton with the coal, the butcher's boy delivered... We had a very good going on [sic], until the War started.' (*Charles Sambrook*). The water supply was variable though, shutting off whenever a steam train stopped at Bradwell Station to fill up – not popular on wash days!

TODAY, WHILE THE view shows little change, around it the new Bradville developed – still
with strong links to the area's past. Nearby Stanton Way was named after a medieval village
deserted in the sixteenth century after imposed clearances for sheep-raising made people's lives
impossible. Other new street names recall Thomas Mercer, owner of Bradwell Manor in 1783;
Sir William Vaux of Vauxhall, lord of Stantonbury Manor in the fifteenth century; and Sir
Nicholas Vaux, after whom Harrowden is named. Sir Nicholas Vaux destroyed Stanton village
and was created Baron of Harrowden only after he was pardoned for his deed.

# STANTONBURY ROAD, NEW BRADWELL

AN EARLY PICTURE of Stantonbury Road *c.*1900. Later known as Newport Road, it was described by the traveller John Hassell in 1819 as: 'a very pleasant road with an abundance of lofty trees.' Forty years later, many of them had to be felled for purpose-built homes for the community of railway workers moving into the area. Evidence of much earlier settlers, from 3,500 years previous, were found in this area, and not only burial mounds but bronze fragments

of tools and weapons, including – as reported in *British Archaeological Report* No. 34 in 1977, a: 'leaf-shaped sword broken into four pieces [in a] deep cist filled with black earth.'

LATER ON, NEWPORT Road provided many local stories for the *Wolverton Express*. Several involved resident Albert Brown, a union activist of the 1926 General Strike when the New Bradwell railway workers – 'Little Moscow' – were considered more militant than Wolverton. Later becoming a councillor and JP, Albert Brown was dramatically rescued when he and his wife nearly drowned in the canal at the bottom of their garden. Today the road recalls its leafier past with the Ouse Valley Park and Recreation Ground (left of the photograph above) and access to the New Bradwell Local Park (right); the chimneypot of Stonebridgehouse Farm can still be seen (centre right).

# THE COUNTY ARMS, CORNER PIN, NEW BRADWELL

THE COUNTY ARMS (photograph *c.*1920, right) is on the bend of the original Newport Road, known as Corner Pin, so named possibly because of a covered bowling alley or 'pin alley' there. Built in 1854, it was much visited by auctioneers, travelling salesmen and concert parties using the nearby assembly hall. By the 1930s dances were held two or three times a week. The Smith family of New Bradwell were invariably involved in such entertainments. 'Piccolo' Smith was a founder member of the Bradwell Silver Band, but his

daughter Nellie was well known for her energetic preparations for the Stantonbury Whitsun Fête, to raise money for Northampton Hospital.

NOW, THE COUNTY Arms, once the largest of the Bradwell pubs and still an imposing building, is undergoing its latest transformation. Once it hosted rock 'n' roll evenings dancing to 'Nick and the Fenders' and provided a venue for the popular local 1960s band 'The Fenton Weils'. Later, the pub's two bars, refurbished from its 1970s style, offered quieter pastimes with darts and pool. But now it is being converted into nine residential flats – planning permission was granted in February 2011. The town's carnival was revived by New Bradwell School in 1986, with the parade led by the indomitable Bradwell Silver Band.

# CORNER PIN, NEWPORT ROAD, NEW BRADWELL

SURVEYING THE CORNER Pin in 1937
(right). The area might well have been so
named because of the sharpness of the
bend. A 1904 traffic census revealed how
busy it was: from 5am to 10pm on a June
day, 6,982 pedestrians were counted,
along with 332 horse-drawn vehicles, 425
bicycles and motors, 361 'perambulators'
and handcarts, 17 horses, 2 donkeys, 1
flock of sheep, 1 steam-threshing outfit
and 3 monkeys! It was calculated that
a straighter road cutting the route by
205yds (200m) would make a difference
of 200 miles a year 'to any person living
in Stantonbury [New Bradwell] and going
home for meals.'

EVENTUALLY, THE ROAD from Wolverton was straightened. More recently, speed bumps
have been added to deter through traffic. The city's twenty-one grid roads, many of them dual
carriageway, have transformed cross-city travel. Its eighty-odd roundabouts without traffic
lights ensure a continuous flow of traffic, even in the 'rush hour' – when to go from one end of a
conurbation of around 200,000 people to the other takes little more than 20 minutes.

The Corner Pin now sits quietly on the border of the 2.5 hectare New Bradwell Local Park, and is
itself alongside a 200m-long open space around the Clock Tower.

# FLOODS AT CORNER PIN,
# NEW BRADWELL

FLOODS AT CORNER Pin, July 1939 (right). Housing here was developed for railway workers' families 1860–1907, but the vagaries of the nearby Bradwell Brook and River Great Ouse made it vulnerable to constant flooding, as the *Wolverton Express* evidences in 1937: 'The Bradwell Brook was much swollen... 23 sheep drowned at Stacey Hill Farm.'; 1939: 'The river rose to 11ft [3.5m] above normal'; 1948: 'Most serious floods...'; 1968: 'A heavy cloudburst on the night of 10th July resulted in the worst flooding for many years. An abnormal rainfall of 4.7 inches [12cm] was recorded in 24 hours.'

NOW, FLOODING IS not a problem, except by a stream of parked cars! The city's ingenious 'balancing lakes'

– eleven of them – are designed as storm-water storage reservoirs, forming a protective girdle around the city, with Bradwell Brook now deepened and straightened. For over forty years, residents have been safeguarded from such disasters as reported in the *Express* in 1968: 'A wall of water raced down Wallace Street. In minutes Newport Road was inundated as the torrent swept on its way through Corner Pin... Over 100 houses were flooded, several elderly residents had to be rescued, [and] other people were marooned in upstairs rooms...'

# HAVERSHAM BRIDGE

HAVERSHAM BRIDGE, (PHOTOGRAPHED in October 1939) crosses the River Great Ouse around half a mile from New Bradwell. The original bridge, built in 1840 following 'an alteration in the railway', consisted of two brick semi-circular and skewed arches, each spanning 33ft 8in (10.5m). In 1938, it was raised and widened at a cost of over £13,000, but just eighteen months later it was washed away, leaving Haversham village isolated: 'Workmen at Wolverton were unable to return for their midday meal... Some climbed the railway embankment and passed over the Viaduct at their own risk...' the *Wolverton Express* reported.

TODAY, HAVERSHAM BRIDGE has extra storm drain arches (behind the trees, right). This view is from the Ouse Valley Park: 'the most rural of any found in Milton Keynes... the feeling of the countryside without leaving the city.' Old trees, hedgerows, meadows, and new plantations combine to provide excellent habitats for wildlife – unlike when, in preparation for the present bridge, hundreds of dead fish resulted from the explosions needed to remove the 250 tons of brick and mortar of the old bridge. 'Some of the fish have been eaten by some men working on the job...' reported the *Wolverton Express* in April 1958.

# THE CUBA HOTEL,
# NEW BRADWELL

THE CUBA HOTEL on Newport Road opened in 1864, and was photographed here for Queen Victoria's Diamond Jubilee (right). Lily Stonton lived there in the early twentieth century as one of fourteen children. Her father, Thomas Giltrow, was landlord for forty-five years. Six brothers fought in the First World War and three sisters were on 'war work'. She recalled Dr Miles being so impressed with her putting a boy's broken leg in a splint that he wanted her to become a nurse, but her father needed her in the pub. Lily also remembered the travelling Penny Gaff where plays were put on in the field opposite.

TODAY, THE CUBA Hotel has lost its imposing main entrance and gained some ornate windows, but it continues to provide entertainment for locals such as darts, pool and karaoke. One customer commented: 'It is a quiet, unassuming pub [with] a TV screen in one room away from the bar that shows football and MTV.' However, live bands – such as Secret Genius ('a contemporary covers band with a bit of edge and attitude'), Shred Belly ('a bunch of blokes who are old enough to know better') and Rufus Stone ('from Punk to the West End, Workingmen's Clubs to Cruises') – raise the tempo.

# NEWPORT ROAD SHOPS, NEW BRADWELL

HARRY LINES' BARBER Shop *c.*1900. Doris Blunt recalled many shops in the New Bradwell of her childhood. Mr Masters, Mr Harrup, Mr Moore and Mr Pearce were bakers 'and they baked our

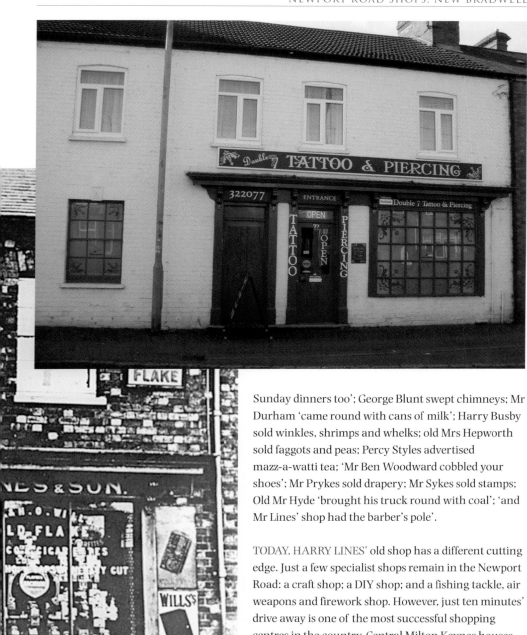

Sunday dinners too'; George Blunt swept chimneys; Mr Durham 'came round with cans of milk'; Harry Busby sold winkles, shrimps and whelks; old Mrs Hepworth sold faggots and peas; Percy Styles advertised mazz-a-watti tea; 'Mr Ben Woodward cobbled your shoes'; Mr Prykes sold drapery; Mr Sykes sold stamps; Old Mr Hyde 'brought his truck round with coal'; 'and Mr Lines' shop had the barber's pole'.

TODAY, HARRY LINES' old shop has a different cutting edge. Just a few specialist shops remain in the Newport Road: a craft shop; a DIY shop; and a fishing tackle, air weapons and firework shop. However, just ten minutes' drive away is one of the most successful shopping centres in the country. Central Milton Keynes houses the centre:mk, Midsummer Place, and the Food Centre – over 250 shops and restaurants all under cover and attracting 30 million visitors a year. In addition there are seven major retail outlets around the city, none of them further than a twenty-minute drive.

53

# NEWPORT ROAD AT THE BRADWELL ROAD JUNCTION, NEW BRADWELL

NEWPORT ROAD LOOKING east at Bradwell Road *c.*1930 (right). The Labour Hall (left of the photograph) was once a shop owned by Mr J.E. Nutt, farrier, blacksmith and wheelwright. Children bought toy iron hoops from him, costing a penny. Reg Mynard remembers it as 'a small engineering firm' near river meadows where horses were put out to pasture. During 1957, the hall played host to the famous 'Rockets', a local rock 'n' roll band led by Terry Carroll (admission 2*s* 6*d* – 12½p). In 1966 the Queen

visited. As her car travelled along Newport Road, the hand-picked brownies and cubs who saluted her were rewarded with only the merest glimpse.

TODAY, NEWPORT ROAD looks more cared for than eight decades ago in, say, 1927 when 338 New Bradwell households were still dependent on wells for water, with gas mains not due to arrive for another eighteen months. In 1965, it cost around £1,500 to buy a terraced house or £3,425 for a detached house. Less than fifty years later, prices seem to have risen a hundred times over, with a terraced house in Newport Road costing £150,000 while the asking price for a detached house is £350,000. Bradwell Road no longer reaches Bradwell Village – unless you use the Redway. Through traffic must travel by grid roads!

# NEWPORT ROAD AT THE GLYN STREET JUNCTION, NEW BRADWELL

GLYN STREET (PHOTOGRAPHED *c.*1920) was named after the first chairman of the London & Birmingham Railway, subsequently of London & North Eastern Railway, George Carr Glyn (1797–1873). A banker and a Liberal Member of Parliament when he was ennobled, he took the title of First Baron Wolverton. He rode with Robert Stephenson on the first through train journey

in September 1838. 'Processions, parades, speeches, flags and bunting were seen at every station... The Board of Directors led by George Carr Glyn really cared for the hundreds [they] employed and the thousands who depended on them for their health, education, and even places of worship,' comments Sir Frank Markham in the *History of Milton Keynes Volume 2*.

THE GLYN STREET junction today is opposite what was once a working men's club (the imposing building to the right of the picture, built in 1919). Now it is a dance school, offering lessons from 'baby-bopping to ballroom'. The small building once next to it has been replaced by modern housing. But it marks nearly 100 years of cycle and motor engineering in the Milton Keynes area. After the family business started up in Somerset in the 1890s, W.G. Sellick developed garages in Wolverton and New Bradwell. In the 1970s the business expanded to new premises in Wolverton from which it still trades.

# QUEEN ANNE STREET, NEW BRADWELL

QUEEN ANNE STREET, photographed here in 1930, saw the inauguration of the New Bradwell's first working men's club on 1 August 1893 before it moved to neighbouring St Giles Street. Stanton's the baker used to be at the junction with Newport Road and children coming home

from New Bradwell School would stand close by the gratings to warm their hands and enjoy the delicious smells. Frank Gostelow's pottery business in the street received a boost in 1937 when the parish council ordered 800 coronation cups and saucers to give to all the schoolchildren of the town.

NOW QUEEN ANNE Street shows the reality of modern car owners living in Victorian terraces. However, it still leads to New Bradwell School in Bounty Street. Originally founded in 1883, this foundation school also serves the modern Blue Bridge estate with around 340 children on roll. The 2008 Ofsted report, addressed to the children, commented: 'We were impressed with your involvement with the local community, and the yearly carnival sounds a really exciting and colourful event.' Organised by the school, the New Bradwell Carnival includes a fête and a parade of themed floats decorated by the children.

# CALEDONIAN ROAD, NEW BRADWELL

CALEDONIAN ROAD IN the snow, 1916. The Sunday school here was known as 'The Tin Hut' according to locals. Between the road and the railway line were the sewage works and rubbish tip – the cause of much heated debate in 1937. Councillor Jeffs declared: 'They must

collect dead cats and dogs! When people in
the vicinity go to bed at nights, the smell
from the burning is enough to poison one.
It's reports, reports, reports – when are
they going to get on with the job and get
something done?' The road's original name
was possibly to acknowledge the *Caledonian
Sleeper* – running on the nearby West Coast
line since 1873.

TODAY, CALEDONIAN ROAD'S thirty-seven
properties are still largely residential (the two
residents on the right arrived there in 1958!)
The road is on the route of the Bradwell Silver
Band's annual carolling event. 'Starting from
the Band room (in New Bradwell School) we
made our way round Queen Anne Street,
King Edward Street, St Giles Street, St Mary
Street, St James Street, Newport Road, Wood
Street, Wallace Street and Caledonian Road.
We had lots of players and were extremely
well received as many people came to their
doors to listen to the band.'

# THE CLOCK TOWER,
# NEW BRADWELL

OPENING CEREMONY FOR Clock Tower Gardens, 1962. This area was once a field where the
Corner Pin Fête took place. It also hosted an annual cycle parade, travelling circuses and fairs
where Giles Thurston's famous fair organ gave recitals of sacred music, while John Sanger's steam

engines used Bradwell Brook's water. When a bandstand was established there in 1903, townsfolk despaired of how young people behaved. Councillor Puryer complained that: 'the cheek of some lads was abominable. One had a carpet fixed between two trees and was swinging on it... and others played on the steps of the bandstand, climbed up the sides and destroyed fences!'

THE CLOCK TOWER Garden today forms a prominent feature of the eastern end of the New Bradwell Local Park. Raised planted beds surrounding the tower are maintained by Milton Keynes Council with most of the rest of the open space being grass interspersed with individual trees. It leads to the Bradwell Brook and new features such as a fenced community orchard and paths connecting the play areas to the central Redway. 'There are provisions for local people of all ages and levels to have the ability to meet, walk sit, play and enjoy.'

# ST MARY'S STREET, NEW BRADWELL

ST MARY'S STREET, here pictured *c.*1930, was open land until around 1890, like neighbouring King Edward Street and St Giles Street. However, more houses were needed to accommodate the swell of new workers migrating from across the country to Wolverton Works. By 1906 the

Works had reached the zenith of its development, covering 80 acres and employing nearly 5,000 people. An internationally renowned leader in industrial development, the Works' power house was the first in the UK to be completely lit and powered electrically in 1901, though the homes housing its workers took a few more decades to catch up.

TODAY, ST MARY'S Street seems little changed except for the parked cars and just one new garage – typical of the little streets in New Bradwell. Television aerials abound too, but the houses seem to have been well cared for. Frederick Church could remember paying rent of 10s (50p) for his St Mary's Street house in the 1930s. By 2011, tenants could expect to pay around £160 per week. Mr Church later bought his house freehold for £110 – when the national average wage was around £200 per annum. In 2011, the prices for such terraced houses ranged from £95,000 to £165,000.

# ST MARY'S STREET CORNER SHOP, NEW BRADWELL

ST MARY'S STREET corner shop (photographed *c.*1970) was used once for collecting parish council rents; it became Dr Love's temporary surgery after the 1940 bombing raid. A prominent local figure, Councillor Dr Love opened the New Bradwell Sports Club – still home now as it was

then to New Bradwell St Peter Football Club; and he and his wife, presidents of the New Bradwell British Legion, unveiled the plaque on Clock Tower memorial. Among those remembered there are two brothers who lived at 67 St Mary's Street – James and John Stallard who both died on 11 November 1914.

THE OLD CORNER shop at the junction of St Mary's Street and St James Street is now a private residence – the result over the last half-century of many such small businesses across the nation giving way to larger stores. However some small shops still trade in New Bradwell. Described on the Milton Keynes Council website as 'a self-contained community with its own churches and chapels, corner shops and pubs', it currently hosts various takeaways providing fish and chips, sandwiches, kebabs and Indian food; a barber's and a beauty shop, several grocers and convenience stores and a few specialist services such as dry-cleaners.

# ST GILES STREET, NEW BRADWELL

ST GILES STREET in the 1930s (below). This picture, like some 2,000 of the Milton Keynes area, was taken by Maurice Kitchener (1894–1969) specifically for local postcards in the 1920s and '30s. He developed and printed the postcards himself and his son David would deliver them

around the villages. The middle son to an Olney factory owner, Maurice created his images on glass plate negatives, now on permanent loan to MK City Discovery Centre. His daughter-in-law Mrs Kitchener allowed some sixteen of the plates to be used for the original version of this book – *Bradwell Past and Present* (1997) – ensuring this precious and unique city resource reached a wider audience.

THE MODERN VIEW of St Giles Street was taken with a digital camera with its instantaneous system of record and recall – a far cry from Maurice Kitchener's travails with a wooden camera strapped to his back, cycling to assignments. From the first ignition of magnesium powder (to light the subject) to the delicate procedures of printing (by shining sunlight through the glass plates onto special coated paper), the photographer eight decades ago had to be a master of timing and patience. St Giles Street now has modern landscaping softening the brick façades – and the ever-present cars.

# STANTONBURY WORKING MEN'S CLUB, NEW BRADWELL

NEW BRADWELL'S WORKING men's club was established on the corner of St Giles and St James Streets in 1885. Named by die-hard locals for 'Stantonbury', the building here was photographed for a picture postcard, sent to Miss Nellie Claridge of 19 Spencer Street on 25 September 1906. The CIU (Club and Institute Union) to which it is affiliated was formed in 1862, headed by the teetotal Revd Henry Solly and supported by members of the aristocracy and high-ranking politicians. They thought working men should have a place to go for 'sober social discourse' after work, to meet friends, relax, read newspapers and books, and perhaps receive patronage and advice.

THE MODERN CLUB has been recently updated, both physically (as can be seen in the modern photograph) and in membership terms: women were granted the right of membership in 2007! Following the ban on smoking in 2009, the club made news when it announced that its takings had actually increased as a result. Club activities have expanded too: there is now a dance floor and lounge and three licensed bars. These would perhaps not have met with the Revd Solly's approval but the various concerts and fundraising events undoubtedly would.

# KING EDWARD STREET, NEW BRADWELL

KING EDWARD STREET jubilee celebrations in 1935. Residents here liked a good street party. Striving to win the council's shield for the best street decoration, they worked from 4am to 9am on Coronation Day 1937. The festivities continued for five days, as reported by the *Wolverton Express*: 'Thousands of people and hundreds of cars passed down the street during the day... Dancing and games were indulged in the street in the evening to music supplied by Mr Baldwin and his fellow bands-men until a late hour.' Less happy were somewhat fraught memories in the street of the 1926 General Strike when neighbours came to blows about the 'blacklegs' who broke the strike.

TODAY, KING EDWARD Street's best-known resident lives on through wonderful stories of his life and experiences. Hawtin Mundy (1894–1985) recorded memories of his life in New Bradwell and at Wolverton Works and his traumatic experiences on the Western Front and since. Hawtin Mundy's remarkable experiences have since spawned, with Living Archive, a community musical documentary play, *Days of Pride*, local and national radio programmes, an award-winning show at the Edinburgh Festival and two books: *I'll Tell You What Happened* and *No Heroes No Cowards*. King Edward Street belies its eventful past with this modern peaceful view.

# ST JAMES STREET,
# NEW BRADWELL

ST JAMES STREET with the church grounds on the left *c.*1975. St James church, part of the planned development by the London & North Western Railway, was designed by G. E. Street, architect of

London's Royal Courts of Justice. It was built in 1858 at a cost of £4,430 and consecrated in 1860. James McConnell, the Works' loco-superintendent, was a very supportive church warden – indeed his son was the first to be baptised there. However, after a bitter dispute with his chairman, Richard Moon, he resigned in 1862. The design had provided for a church tower, but when McConnell left, interest in the project waned and it was never built.

THE QUIET NORMALITY of St James Street today belies the colourful activities of past characters that endure. For example, the bizarre life of a local priest 'Joey' Guest, vicar of St James for nearly thirty-eight years until 1946, lives on not only in his own literary creation but also in documentary theatre. Revd Allan Newman Guest published his *Stantonbury Tales* in 1924 with gothic relish, describing in one part of the account 'a terrible face with protruding eyes and coal-like visage'; and *The Jovial Priest*, a musical community play produced by Living Archive, showed how 'Joey' Guest provoked the choir to strike and denounced his congregation as having married illegally and living in sin!

# OLD SCHOOL BUILDINGS, NEW BRADWELL

SCHOOLCHILDREN AT THE Church Street entrance to the school, 1908, pictured on a postcard dated 26 September 1908 with a message to Mrs Day in South Devon: 'Leslie is one of the Assistants and these are some of the boys.' The school was built next to the church, and the *Illustrated London News* reported in 1856 that it was 'for the instruction of girls, boys and an infant school [100 of each]... with dwellings for masters and/or mistresses.' A pupil in 1908 described

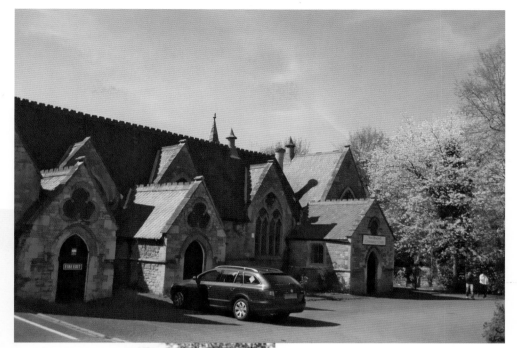

how the children were each charged a penny a week for lead pencil and slate, and that the teacher would nudge pupils with his pointer to see if they were awake!

THE BUILDINGS TODAY are used for the New Bradwell Community Centre and workshops. Designed like the church by G.E. Street in 1858, they were renovated by Milton Keynes Development Corporation in 1978. The New Bradwell Heritage Group, formed in 2005, meets there to research and digitally record the history of New Bradwell for the local community and future generations. The group arranges such events as the Sesquicentury (150 years) Celebrations 1858–2008 when there were talks, quizzes, poetry readings, exhibitions, a fair, music and dancing – and local schoolchildren experienced authentic Victorian lessons for themselves in the old schoolroom.

# ST JAMES STREET, BOUNTY STREET AND HIGH STREET JUNCTION, NEW BRADWELL

THE TOP OF St James Street in the 1930s: the corner shop (left) has reportedly transformed over the years from a stable (complete with horse in the 1900s), a draper (1920–30s), a confectioner and tobacconist (1970s) to a barber (1990s). Geoff Lines can remember being sent there by his headmaster in the 1960s to buy him his Embassy cigarettes! Other traders in the street included

Lloyds Fancy Goods, Woods Sweet Shop and Wheelers Shoes; 'We always bought our shoes from Wheelers. The walls packed with boxes of shoes; it was difficult to choose which we wanted,' Jennifer Cooper remembers. The boy in the foreground is thought to be the photographer's son, David Kitchener.

TODAY ST JAMES Street still has a number of specialist small traders – including suppliers of kitchen furniture, glazing and blinds, a printer's, a recording studio and funeral services. But one recent business that operated in the street at least until 2004 was the Bronze Foundry, a nationally acclaimed sculpting partnership that has supplied some of Milton Keynes' most notable public artworks. 'Dream Flight', 'High Flyer' and 'Flying Carpet' were commissioned by Milton Keynes Development Corporation in 1989 for open-air display on Queens Court in Central Milton Keynes. They were subsequently donated to Milton Keynes Council.

# HIGH STREET, NEW BRADWELL

HIGH STREET AT the junction with Church Street, *c.*1950. The High Street was the main site of the railway cottages (seen on the right of the photograph) demolished by Wolverton Urban

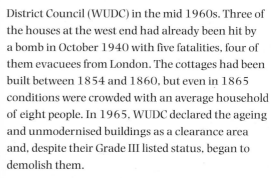

District Council (WUDC) in the mid 1960s. Three of the houses at the west end had already been hit by a bomb in October 1940 with five fatalities, four of them evacuees from London. The cottages had been built between 1854 and 1860, but even in 1865 conditions were crowded with an average household of eight people. In 1965, WUDC declared the ageing and unmodernised buildings as a clearance area and, despite their Grade III listed status, began to demolish them.

TODAY THE SOUTH (right) side of the High Street has been replaced by the modern residential development of Permayne, built in the mid 1980s. (The name may derive from 'permain' or 'pearmain' – a type of winter apple or baking pear.) The scheme includes three-storey townhouses on the High Street side and a wide-open green space in front where once there were terraces and narrow pavements – and shadows from the old buildings falling over the road nearly all day. A sheltered housing scheme is also part of the new development, with the Redways and the Grand Union Canal accessed nearby.

# HIGH STREET PARADE,
# NEW BRADWELL

HIGH STREET PARADE, 1909. The Bradwell Silver Band leads children along High Street, New Bradwell on their way to Wolverton Works' Canteen for the annual Co-op Guild Day Tea Party. Mr Casebrook, manager of the High Street Grocery Branch, heads the procession with thirteen members of the band following. Among them is William Baker (fourth bandsman from left, wearing a cap). A resident of Thompson Street, he was killed six years later in the Great War aged twenty-seven, leaving a wife and family. Another, Dave Johnson (second bandsman from right) might be Sgt D. Johnson of New Bradwell who also died.

HIGH STREET PARADES are still undertaken by the Bradwell Silver Band – which has now been in 'continuous existence' for over a century, since 1 January 1901. Most of the original members worked for the railway company in Wolverton, though with the Works ceasing to be a major employer in the 1980s, current membership is 'drawn from a cross-section of trades and professions'. The terrace of houses fronting this west end of the High Street seems to have been carefully renovated and now faces a green open space instead of a looming bank of red-brick railway terraces directly opposite.

# HIGH STREET,
# NEW BRADWELL
# FROM THE EAST END

THIS HIGH STREET view photographed in the 1930s shows how close the facing terraces were to each other, and how narrow the pavements. In 1851, the population of Stantonbury, as it was known then, was 351. By 1861 there were 1,658 inhabitants living in 200 new houses with 46 local businesses operating. The *Illustrated London News* commented: 'The cottages are

remarkably neat in appearance and are built in the most substantial manner with regard to every comfort and convenience.' By 1871, the population had grown to 2,409; ten years later it was 2,906; and by 1900 a total of 3,512 people lived in the new community.

THE HIGH STREET today comprises thirty-seven properties, most of them residential. At the 2001 census, the population of the New Bradwell parish was 2,990; that of MK13, which is the New Bradwell postcode, is nearly 18,000, but this includes all the areas covered by this book as well as Stony Stratford and Wolverton. The average age of residents was thirty-four with a third of them being single and a fifth living in rented housing – the majority of housing being owner-occupied. Over a third of the housing is still in terraces – 'the most significant proportion' – yet now without the crowded conditions experienced by families 100 years ago.

# SPENCER STREET, NEW BRADWELL

THE ORIGINAL SPENCER Street looking east
*c.*1965 (right). Spencer Street ran parallel to the full
length of the High Street. Here is the hierarchical
and ordered nature of Victorian industrial society:
the small two-storey terraces were for the workers
with the three-storey pavilion end-terraces for the
foremen. Each plot was 8 x 16yds (7m x 15m) –
thought to be very spacious. Fireplaces were set in
one corner with the cooking range in the kitchen
– to be black-leaded every morning, with the hearth

whitened, the front step scrubbed, the pavement washed, the front room fireplace polished with Brasso, and the steel fire-irons rubbed with emery paper.

THE SPENCER STREET railway cottages were listed Grade III and subject to a public enquiry in 1975, though only after most of the street, along with all the Bridge Street cottages, was demolished. Just this last small section in the left-hand photograph survived. They were purchased by Milton Keynes Development Corporation and restored in 1978 and later became known as the Rainbow Housing Co-operative. Today, this leafy pedestrianised street stands as testament to how old properties can become beautiful modern homes, and how bad decisions on demolition cannot be retracted. As Geoff Lines said on leaving his home in Bridge Street: 'It was lovely in them little streets...'

# BRADWELL ROAD CANAL BRIDGE, NEW BRADWELL

LOOKING DOWN BRADWELL Road from the canal bridge *c.* 1930. The original Bridge Street (left) marked the eastern limit of the homes built for the London North Western Railway. The earlier tollgate house, built in 1816, was originally at the foot of the hill where it met Newport Road. Later this was known as Busby's Corner: Bert and Harry Busby sold cockles, mussels, oysters, shrimps, winkles and whelks from their cart. The cart also doubled up as a corpse-carrier for when suicides or drunks were retrieved from the canal. Most famously of all, the Revd Guest was known to race down the hill on his bicycle shouting 'Get out of the way!'

THE VIEW FROM the bridge today shows a
quite different perspective on the left, where
the new city development of Permayne has
replaced the old railway terraces of Bridge
Street. But the view of the countryside beyond
seems little changed: the River Great Ouse still
flows through its water meadows, though it is
now alongside the seven lakes of former gravel
workings – Randall, Haversham and Little
Linford Lakes on its left bank and Bradwell,
Stantonbury, Blackhorse and Redhouse Lakes on
its right. Local buses squeeze past the bollards on
their way up the hill through to city centre and
Bletchley beyond.

# THE NEW INN

THE NEW INN, photographed *c.*1920, is one of New Bradwell's oldest buildings. Built in 1804 as the Wharf Inn, it was advertised for sale in 1828 with: 'a large and commodious Wharf, Stables for 30 horses, Corn Granaries, Coke and Salt Houses, Pigsties, Brewhouse, Wash-house, Offices, a large garden, a good Well of water and cellarage for 100 hogsheads [250,000 litres]... a most compact and desirable residence.' Despite the description, it became known as the War Office because of its riotous reputation from visiting railway navvies. One landlord was advised that if he couldn't throw customers out through the door, he should throw them out of the window!

TODAY THE NEW Inn is an award-winning
pub, popular for its extensive gardens on the
canal side and moorings for boats. After major
refurbishment in 2006, it boasted a panelled
snug in the lounge bar, a public bar with log
burner and wooden floors and a restaurant. It is a
Grade II listed building, distinguished by its three
roof ridges, its gables on the roadside, original
windows and slate roof. Instead of being on a
vital trade route with narrowboats transporting
coal and goods from London to Birmingham, it
is now visited by leisure craft and their attendant
ducks, geese and swans.

# CANAL BRIDGE, NEW BRADWELL

THE FORMER CANAL bridge at New Bradwell, looking west, 1938. The canal was originally called Grand Junction, but in 1929 became part of the Grand Union Company. From its opening in 1805 until the railways forced its commercial demise, the canal had varying commodities gliding along: sand, gravel, roadstone, bricks, manure, milk, coconut oil and ale. In 1806, a

record load of 100 bemused sheep passed by from Northampton, taking more than two days to get to London. Sometimes sixteen horses would be towing a barge – with old tins or boots tied behind them to make them think they were accompanied!

THE NEW BRIDGE is thought to have been built *c.*1950 after the hill on Bradwell Road continued to cause problems for the increasing traffic. The severe winter of 1947 created twenty-two degrees of frost that prevented omnibuses from climbing it and cyclists from riding down it, and 'pedestrians clung desperately to railings to prevent themselves from falling', according to the *Wolverton Express*. The approach was subsequently levelled out but at the cost of replacing the picturesque old rounded stone bridge with the current rectangular brick one. Just before the bridge – numbered 72 – is a privately constructed dry dock in the back garden of a house (left).

# BRADWELL STATION, BETWEEN WOLVERTON AND NEWPORT PAGNELL

THIS FAMOUS POSTCARD picture of Bradwell Station c.1910 shows the LNWR tank engine No. 58887, arriving from Wolverton on what was known locally as the 'Nobby' line – just 4 miles long. The first engine ran in 1865 when it hauled seventeen wagons, which were, according to Arthur Griggs, 'crammed with navvies'. The line opened for public service in 1867 and ran for nearly 100 years. Among its first stationmasters was Henry Roddis (1887); among its last, Albert West, who served from 1949 to 1961.

He issued and collected tickets, balanced accounts, cleaned the station and in his spare time would deliver parcels to the neighbouring community.

TODAY, JUST THE platform of the old station remains. The last passenger train ran on 7 September 1964. Goods traffic continued for three years until May 1967. The track was lifted the same year, but the track-bed has been reincarnated as a modern Redway for cyclists and pedestrians, part of the extensive purpose-built network in Milton Keynes. It is on the route of Heritage Trail A: a 10-mile city-wide circular trail which starts at Willen Lake and includes Great Linford (another station site) as well as Blue Bridge, Bancroft, Bradwell Village, Bradwell Abbey... in fact it is the perfect tour for seeing many of the places covered in this book!

Other titles published by The History Press

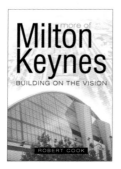

## More of Milton Keynes, Building on the Vision
ROBERT COOK

Milton Keynes has been designated one of the four potential growth areas in the south-east of England. There are plans to build up to 70,000 new homes in the city before 2031, and also develop transport infrastructure. Here, Robert Cook examines the history of Milton Keynes so far, and also explores surrounding towns and villages.

978 0 7509 3859 4

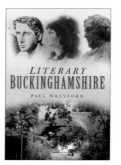

## Literary Buckinghamshire
PAUL WREYFORD

Poet John Betjemen was not the only scribe 'beckoned out to lanes in beechy Bucks'. Many of the country's most famous writers shared his fondness for the county and sought solace within its boundaries. John Milton came here to escape the plague in London; Enid Blyton fled the capital's increasing development, while D.H. Lawrence and his German wife took refuge on the outbreak of the First World War.

978 0 7509 4959 0

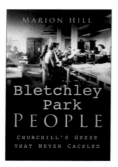

## Bletchley Park People
MARION HILL

The British government's top secret Code & Cypher School at Bletchley Park, otherwise known as Station X, was the unlikely setting for one of the most vital undercover operations of the Second World War. It was at Bletchley in present-day Milton Keynes that teams of code breakers succeeded in cracking Germany's supposedly unbreakable Enigma codes, shortening the war by at least two years. A selection of intriguing archive photographs and illustrations accompanies.

978 0 7509 3362 9

## Buckingham Voices
ROBERT COOK

Through careful and meticulous collection Robert Cook has documented the changes in family circumstances, daily work and social experiences of the people of Buckingham, both public and private, as made readily available in their own words. This book is a unique record for the historian and will also appeal to a varitiety of generations who wish to recall times past.

978 0 7524 2198 8

Visit our website and discover thousands of other History Press books.

**www.thehistorypress.co.uk**